ROCK EXPLORER

ROCKS

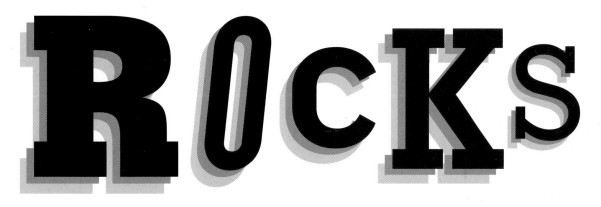

Claudia Martin

Quarto is the authority on a wide range of topics.

Quarto educates, entertains and enriches the lives of our readers—enthusiasts and lovers of hands-on living.

www.quartoknows.com

Editor: Clare Hibbert
Designer: Dave Ball

First Published in 2017 by QED Publishing,
an imprint of The Quarto Group.
The Old Brewery, 6 Blundell Street,
London N7 9BH, United Kingdom.
T (0)20 7700 6700 F (0)20 7700 8066
www.QuartoKnows.com

A catalogue record for this book is available from the British Library.

ISBN 978-1-78493-965-6

Manufactured in Guangdong, China TT022018

9 8 7 6 5 4 3 2 1

MIX
Paper from
responsible sources
FSC® C016973
FSC
www.fsc.org

Contents

What is a Rock?

There are hundreds of types of rock. Some are hard, some are crumbly – and some are very strange!

This tower is made of a rock called sandstone. It is in Arizona, USA.

ROCKY PLANET

Rock covers our planet. In some places bare rock is visible, but rock also lies under cities, soil and oceans.

Rock families

There are three kinds of rock: igneous, sedimentary and metamorphic. Each kind forms in a different way.

Igneous

Sedimentary

Metamorphic

▼ Granite is an igneous rock that contains different coloured minerals.

MINERAL MIXTURES

Rocks are mixtures of different minerals. Minerals grow in the ground or in water. They are solids.

Igneous **Rock**

Deep inside the Earth is hot, runny rock called magma. When magma cools, it hardens to form igneous rock.

ERUPTION!

Some igneous rocks form when magma bursts onto the Earth's surface.

When magma erupts from a volcano it is called lava. ▶

Obsidian forms when magma erupts from a volcano, then cools very fast.

Underground activity

Not all igneous rocks form at the surface. Gabbro is created when magma cools underground.

Gabbro

Pumice forms when bubbly magma is thrown from a volcano.

The Giant's Causeway is made of slabs of basalt. The basalt formed when runny magma cooled and cracked.

ROUTE ACROSS THE SEA

According to legend, a giant built the Giant's Causeway in Northern Ireland. He needed to cross the sea to fight a Scottish giant.

Sedimentary
Rock

Sedimentary rocks are made when pebbles, minerals or dead animals and plants are pressed together.

◀ Chalk is a soft, crumbly rock.

WHITE CLIFFS
Chalk is made from seashells that collected on the seabed. After millions of years, they hardened into rock.

LAYER ON LAYER

Look for layers of different materials in sedimentary rocks. Sandstone is pressed sand. Mudstone and shale are pressed mud.

◄ These stripes are layers of sandstone and mudstone.

ON THE MOVE

Earth is covered by massive, slow-moving plates of rock. They push land together or pull it apart. What was once seabed can end up far inland.

▼ These pointed pieces of limestone formed from shells and corals. The area is now a desert!

Metamorphic
Rock

Any rock can change into metamorphic rock.
All it takes is great heat or pressure.

MOVING PLATES

Rock sometimes comes under pressure from the movement of Earth's plates. This can squash or fold the rock.

▼ This metamorphic rock, schist, has been bent and folded.

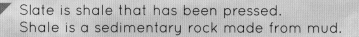

Slate is shale that has been pressed.
Shale is a sedimentary rock made from mud.

HEATING UP

Many metamorphic rocks are made when rocks get very hot. This can happen deep inside the Earth.

The metamorphic rock marble is limestone that has been heated. Its swirling colours are made by minerals in the limestone.

Precious gems

Some metamorphic rocks contain secrets. Precious gems can grow from minerals trapped in the super-hot rock.

This ruby formed inside a slab of marble.

Amazing
Patterns

Some rocks are striped or lumpy.
The patterns tell us how the
rocks were made.

BRILLIANT BANDS
Stripes can form in
metamorphic rocks.
It happens when
pressing, sliding or
heat separate the
different minerals
in the rock.

Gneiss has stripes of dark
and light minerals.

UNUSUAL SURFACES

Sedimentary rocks often form with lumps and bumps.

Mineral grains called ooliths settled on this limestone.

Conglomerate is mudstone or sandstone with pebbles trapped in it.

ANCIENT LIFE FORMS

Some sedimentary rocks are patterned with fossils.

Ferns were preserved in this sandstone.

Rainbow mountains

The striped mountains in Danxia, China, are made of different-coloured sandstones. The layers were pushed and turned by the Earth's plates.

Strange
Shapes

Wind, rain and rivers can rub rocks into weird shapes. This is called erosion.

AMAZING ARCHES
Arches can form when wind and water wear away soft rock. Harder rock is left behind.

Carved canyon

The Grand Canyon in Arizona, USA, is 446 km long. It was worn away by the Colorado River.

STUNNING STACKS

Waves and wind can wear cliffs into towers called stacks. The Twelve Apostles are limestone stacks off the coast of Australia.

Only eight of the ▼ Twelve Apostles are left.

FAIRY CHIMNEYS

Odd pillars of rock are sometimes called fairy chimneys or hoodoos.

▲ A sandstone arch in Utah, USA

▼ Fairy chimneys in central Turkey

▼ Hoodoos in Utah, USA

Deep **Caves**

Deep, dark caves can be found underground.
They are worn away by water.

DISSOLVING ROCK

When rainwater or water from an underground river soaks into limestone, the rock dissolves. Tiny grains of rock mix with the water and are carried away.

These limestone caves are in Slovenia. ▶

Some minerals dangle from the ceiling as stalactites.

DRIP, DRIP

Water containing the dissolved minerals drips into the cave. It leaves some minerals behind.

Some minerals collect below a dripping stalactite. They build up into towers called stalagmites.

Useful **Rock**

Humans have used rocks for thousands of years. There are useful rocks everywhere!

STONE AGE
Before people knew how to work with metal, they used hard rocks to make weapons and tools.

BUILDING BLOCKS
Strong, sturdy rock can create beautiful buildings.

India's Taj Mahal is built from marble.

Stone Age people carved arrowheads from rock.

FOSSIL FUEL

Coal is a sedimentary rock made of plants that died millions of years ago.

▲ Coal is burnt as a fuel.

▲ Gravel helps water to drain away.

GREAT GRAVEL

Pieces of rock, called gravel, are used to build roads.

Deepest mine

Miners dig into rocks to find useful minerals, such as gold and salt. The deepest mines go several kilometres into the ground.

Rock **Art**

Rocks can be turned into amazing art.
They can be carved, moulded or painted.

SUPER SAND

Sand is found on beaches and in deserts, where waves or wind break rock into little pieces.

Buddhist monks used coloured sand to make this mandala.

STONE CARVING

It takes years of practice to carve stone into statues or furniture.

▼ This sculptor is using a chisel to carve stone.

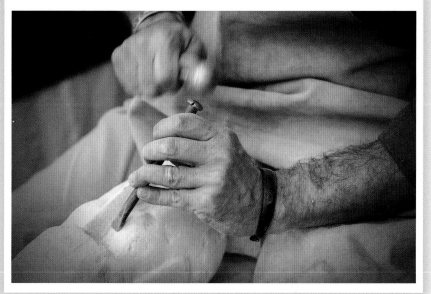

Around 40,000 years ago, humans started to paint the walls of caves. They often drew the animals they hunted.

▲ Lascaux Cave, France

▼ After clay is shaped, it can be hardened by heating it.

PERFECT POTS

Clay is a soft rock. It was formed from plants and minerals mixed with water.

Rock
Guide

BASALT
Type: Igneous
Description: Dark grey and hard

CHALK
Type: Sedimentary
Description: White, soft and crumbly

CLAY
Type: Sedimentary
Description: White to brownish-orange; soft when wet

COAL
Type: Sedimentary
Description: Brown or black; easy to burn

CONGLOMERATE
Type: Sedimentary
Description: Rounded pebbles cemented into sandstone or mudstone

GRANITE
Type: Igneous
Description: Grey or pinkish with grains of coloured minerals

LIMESTONE
Type: Sedimentary
Description: Grey to yellowish; slowly dissolves in rainwater

MARBLE
Type: Metamorphic
Description: White or pink to blue, green or black; can have swirling patterns

OBSIDIAN
Type: Igneous
Description: Dark, very hard and shiny

PUMICE
Type: Igneous
Description: Pale, full of holes and lightweight

SANDSTONE
Type: Sedimentary
Description: Sand-coloured, from white to black; rough and grainy

SLATE
Type: Metamorphic
Description: Usually grey; easy to split into flat sheets

Glossary

dissolves Mixes in with water or another liquid.

erosion Wearing away by wind, water or ice.

fossil The remains of an animal or plant that lived long ago, pressed into rock or turned into rock.

fuel A material that is burnt to make heat.

gemstone A beautiful and hard mineral or rock that is used in jewellery.

igneous rock Rock formed when magma cools down and hardens.

magma Hot, runny rock that lies beneath Earth's surface of cool, hardened rock.

mandala A round picture that represents the universe for Hindus or Buddhists.

metamorphic rock Rock formed when any type of rock is changed by heat or pressure.

mineral A solid formed in the ground or in water.

plate One of the giant slabs of rock that make up the surface of the Earth.

pressure A pressing force.

rock A solid made from different minerals.

sedimentary rock Rock formed when sand, mud, minerals or plant and animal remains are pressed together until they harden.

Index

24

PICTURE CREDITS